DANIEL
AND
HIS VERY GOOD FRIEND
by Sunny Griffin

Illustrated by Linda Welty

King Darius was
a very good
friend to Daniel?

DID YOU KNOW...

There were bad men in the kingdom who didn't want Daniel and King Darius to be good friends?

They talked
King Darius into
making a new law
that everyone had
to pray to him?

Daniel broke the law
because he would
not pray to
anyone but God?

DID YOU KNOW...
Because Daniel
broke the law,
King Darius had
him thrown into
a pit of big,
hungry lions?

DID YOU KNOW...
Daniel prayed to
God asking him to be
saved from the
mouths of the big,
hungry lions?

God heard
Daniel's prayer and
sent an angel to
close the big, hungry
lions' mouths?

King Darius could
not sleep that night
because he was
so sorry for
what he had done
to his very good
friend Daniel?

The next morning King Darius hurried to the pit where the big, hungry lions were kept?

King Darius was
overjoyed when
his very good friend
Daniel came out
of the pit?

DID YOU KNOW...
He was so happy
that he changed the
law so everyone
would pray to
Daniel's God?

DID YOU KNOW...
Daniel and King Darius remained very good friends and worshipped God together for the rest of their lives.

King Darius found the bad men who talked him into making the wrong law. He had them thrown into the lion's pit!

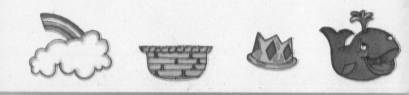